# Guide to Forgiveness Meditation

*An Effective Method to Dissolve Blocks to Loving-Kindness and Living in the Present*

Bhante Vimalaramsi

Other Books by Bhante Vimalaramsi:

| | |
|---|---|
| *A Guide to Tranquil Wisdom Insight Meditation* | 2016 |
| *Meditation is Life, Life is Meditation* | 2014 |
| *The Dhamma Leaf Series* | 2014 |
| *Moving Dhamma Vol 1.* | 2012 |
| *Breath of Love* | 2011 |
| *Anapanasati Sutta* | 1998-2003 |

*"There is no question that Forgiveness Meditation is part of Loving-Kindness Meditation development.*

*It is the first step towards Peace."*

# Table of Contents

# Acknowledgement

This booklet was based on a talk I gave in 2012 at DSMC. It was done with the intention of making a video for the internet concerning my basic technique of working with Forgiveness in meditation. This talk is on our web site.

I wish to acknowledge Ven. Sister Khema's hard work in transcribing this talk, for seeing and conceiving a potential book, for her primary editing, and offering her own additions and advice during final editing. I also wish to thank a dearly departed Dhamma supporter, Dr. Otha Wingo for his contributions in helping to improve the clarity of this subject into a format for easier reading. This was a great contribution for us all. And David for final editing and publishing in book form.

# *Foreword*

When Ven. Sister Khema requested me to write a forward to this booklet I accepted the invitation with considerable pleasure since I esteem being associated with this literary endeavor of unusual significance and immense practical relevance.

It is common knowledge that a large number of books and other literary works have been published on the subject of all aspects of meditative practices leading to 'Loving Kindness Meditation'. The less discerning public might wonder 'why another booklet on the same subject'. The author perhaps anticipating such hesitation and misgiving has stated the principal objective of this booklet in very clear and precise terms. Without being far too exhaustive, highly specialized or too scholarly to be of much practical help to the uninstructed and uninitiated or even to the average person seeking basic concise guidance, the author has provided us a brief, clear and simple handbook which is a much-felt need. Even a cursory glance of the booklet should make it clear that this booklet is an entirely fresh orchestration of most of the salient issues of Forgiveness Meditation.

Often the author's language is unusually illustrative. For instance here is a classic example: "....we can clear the runway for our Mindfulness of Loving-Kindness to take off by first learning to use Mindfulness of Forgiveness meditation. This is an extremely powerful cleansing practice." (Page 8)

The Buddha's supreme and timeless proclamation of liberation of thought and the prioritization of the mind over twenty-five centuries ago is now universally accepted by modern day scientists. As humanity advances and with intellectual development, the quest for spiritual solace enhances this advancement. The author clearly indicates the principal and unique feature of the discipline of the mind through meditation.

This booklet shows in clear and simple terms the way towards spiritual cleansing and dispelling psychic irritants. A commendable feature of this booklet is that the treatment is basic but very precise and comprehensive. I have no doubt whatsoever that this booklet will help the readers towards meaningful practice of 'Forgiveness Meditation' leading to the successful practice of 'Loving-Kindness Meditation'.

*"Bhavatu Sabba Mangalam !"*
May you have All Good Blessings!

Ven. H. Kondañña, Abbot
Staten Island Buddhist Vihara

# Introduction

The Buddha was a meditation teacher. He taught meditation for 45 years after he became fully awakened. When you study and practice meditation you will not be entirely successful until you master the definitions and interwoven nature of two words. Meditation and Mindfulness. I can give you the definitions but then you must experience for yourself how these two work together.

In the Buddhist teachings, Meditation means, 'observing the movement of mind's attention moment-to-moment, in order to see clearly how the links Dependent Origination actually work.' Mindfulness means 'remembering to observe '<u>How</u>' mind's attention moves from one thing to another. This use of mindfulness actually causes mind to become sharper as you go as you experience more subtle states of mind. It isn't hard to see why you must develop this precise mindfulness to keep the meditation going smoothly.

Many people practice Loving-Kindness meditation, but, according to a few people, the power of it doesn't seem to change much for them in their daily lives. If it doesn't take off quite right in the beginning, we might run into difficulty with this practice and it can be like hitting a wall. It's good to know that there is a key to the solution for developing metta in our daily activities. That solution is learning to smile as much as you can remember.

Apparently, in some cases, if we do get into trouble, we can clear the runway for our Mindfulness of Loving-Kindness to take off by first learning to use Mindfulness of Forgiveness meditation. This is an extremely powerful and cleansing practice. Forgiveness is a form of loving-kindness that really clears our mind of negative or unwholesome states.

The reason this book came into being is because of the many questions teachers are asked about 'why doesn't my Mettā arise easily?'. It is because we need to forgive ourselves first before we can send out pure love to others.

# *CHAPTER ONE - Preparation*

**At times,** there can be confusion about how to effectively practice this Mindfulness of Forgiveness meditation. So, this booklet is dedicated only to this meditation on forgiveness so you can begin the practice with a clear goal and better understanding.

When people are practicing Loving-Kindness Meditation, you might run into a barrier as you try to send out Loving-Kindness to yourself and to others. If this happens after a few days, and you are not successful in feeling the metta in the retreat, it may be suggested for you to take a step back and start doing the Forgiveness Meditation to overcome these blocks. After all, we cannot sincerely send Loving-kindness and Forgiveness to someone else when we do not have it for ourselves. This practice is not just used for a person pursuing Loving-Kindness and Compassion meditation. Any person can make the commitment to clean house by doing this forgiveness work. After this is done for the first time, one feels many years younger, because often times, a great weight has been lifted off your heart and mind.

Some people have the idea that this meditation is a completely different kind of meditation from the Loving-

Kindness meditation. That is not so. It should be made clear from the beginning that the Forgiveness Meditation is not outside of the development of Loving-Kindness and is a part of metta. For anyone who has difficulty in feeling loving-kindness, this can be the first step. It creates a firm bridge between heart and mind that is then used to help all other kinds of meditation succeed. It is a cleansing for the heart: another opening of the heart we can add to our initial practice of Generosity.

In truth, this meditation is probably the most powerful meditation that I know. It can clear away mental blocks that pop up from old attachments or dislikes towards various people, or events that happened to you in your past life experiences. If you follow directions closely, and you are patient when you practice, then pain and suffering will gradually dissolve any hard-heartedness you still carry in your mind, about past life wounds.

When you practice Forgiveness meditation, all of the basic rules will remain the same. You still sit in a reasonably quiet space to do this work. Be sure you are wearing loose comfortable clothing. Sit in a comfortable position, on the floor or in a chair. If you do use a chair, don't lean into the back of the chair. Sit with your spine nicely straight but not tightly erect. Sit in a position that does not bring up physical pain in general for you. You should follow the basics of practicing Right Effort using Tranquil Wisdom Insight Meditation (TWIM) and the 6Rs for your meditation cycle to accomplish your goal.

When you practice, sit for a minimum of 30 minutes each time. Sit longer if things are going smoothly and you have the time. At whatever time you decide to break your sitting, stand up slowly. Keep your observation going as you stand up. Stretch slowly if desired.

While you are sitting, do not move at all. Don't wiggle your toes, don't scratch. If your body needs to cough or sneeze, do not hold this in; just sneeze or cough! Keep some tissues close by for any tears that might arise. If tears do fall, then let them come. That is what you have holes in your eyelids for... So, let the tears come out. This releases the pressure. Consider this the cleansing time before you take up any other primary meditations.

While practicing Forgiveness meditation, please use ONLY these meditation instructions and put all other meditation instructions aside until you have completed the work. This just means that we don't want to confuse mind, so, don't mix up the recipe! We want only the information needed to do this practice.

# CHAPTER TWO - Instructions

**The way you start** practicing forgiveness meditation is by forgiving yourself.

There are different kinds of statements that you can use for this to help bring up any old grudges and hardheartedness locked inside you. You may pick one statement to begin and then you stay with that statement for a period of time, to give it a chance to settle in and you and see what comes up. The first suggested phrase is **"I forgive myself for not understanding."** Everybody has misunderstandings that happen in their life. Nobody is exempt from this fact.

**While you are sitting** you repeat the phrase, "I forgive myself for not understanding". After you've done that, you put that feeling into your heart and stay with that feeling of forgiveness. When that feeling fades away or the mind gets distracted, then you come back and forgive yourself for not understanding again. If you are familiar with the 6R process you should 6R any distractions arise. The appendix has a large section on how you practice the 6Rs.

For those familiar with the Jhanas, and have meditated before, it is necessary to not go higher than the first jhana.

You can't mentally verbalize beyond that (say your phrases for forgiveness). Please make a determination to not go any deeper. This is an active contemplative process that we are doing now.

While you're doing this, your mind is going to have some resistance to this meditation. Your mind is going to take off and say, "Well, this is stupid! I shouldn't be doing this! Reactions like these are part of your attachments. These are the obstacles that we must dissolve.

Stay with your statement and repeat, "I forgive myself for not understanding".   Then your mind might say, "AAH! I don't need to do this anymore. This meditation doesn't work".  Every thought that pulls you away from forgiving yourself for not understanding is an attachment and has to be let go and the tension and tightness in that attachment must be "relaxed" away.

This is where you use the 6R's you learned with your basic Metta meditation practice. The 6R's are Recognize‹ Release ‹ Relax ‹ Re-Smile › Return › Repeat. That is the entire cycle.  You RECOGNIZE that mind is distracted. You RELEASE the distraction by not keeping your attention on it.  You RELAX the tightness in your head and heart and you RE-SMILE; and then you softly come back to the statement and you stay with the statement for as long as you can. If you are distracted again you repeat the process.

It doesn't matter how many times your mind gets distracted. One thing that many people get caught with is getting wrapped up in the story about things and this can cause lots of pain and suffering along with some frustration. The 6R's will help you to see how strong the attachments are and it shows the way to overcome the suffering they cause. Recognize it. Let it be. Relax. Smile. Come back and stay with the feeling of forgiveness for as long as you can.

Sitting should be followed by Walking Practice. If you are going to continue sitting again, or you are going to return to a task in daily life, before you do, take a stroll, at a normal pace to keep your blood flowing nicely. Walk for about 15 minutes minimum in some fresh air. 45 minutes is a good maximum time for walking. If you are working in a restricted space setting, find a space that is level and at least 30 feet long in length. Walk back and forth, and mentally, keep your meditation going.

**\*When you walk** you want to walk in a way that you repeat the phrases with each stride as you walk. Like this - with the left foot take a step and mentally say "I" then a right step **"forgive"** and left say **"you"**. Then again, but say, **"You"** on the right step, and then left step, **"forgive"**, right step, **"me"**. And repeat. Back and forth. It can get into a nice cadence but all the while it is really getting it into your 'noggin' to forgive! "I forgive you, you forgive me". And keep smiling when you are doing this. And 6R anything or anyone who comes up. Stay with the walking. I used to go for 6-8 mile walks in Hawaii doing just this practice!

The idea of sitting and walking is to create a continuous flow of meditation without stopping. This proves you can keep the meditation with you all the time in life. While walking at this normal pace, continue doing the forgiveness meditation with your eyes looking down towards the ground about 6 or 7 feet in front of you.  Do not look around.  Keep on gently forgiving.  Keep smiling all the time.

# CHAPTER THREE - Attachments

One mistake that an awful lot of people make is they say, "Well, meditation is just for sitting. The rest of the time I don't have anything else to do, so, I can let my mind act like it always does." This is a mistake. We need to consider the idea that Meditation is life and Life is meditation. You want to realize that you have attachments in your daily life and just because you are not sitting doesn't mean those attachments aren't there. The whole point in doing the meditation is for personality development. It's for letting go of old habitual suffering [bhava}, and in place of this, developing a mind that has equanimity in it.

The more resistance your mind has in doing this, the more you need to do it, because the resistance is your mind showing you where your attachment is, and that is the cause of suffering. This meditation works better than anything that I know of for letting go of attachments, letting go and relaxing of old hard-hearted feelings [bhava], letting go of the way you think the world is supposed to be, so you can start accepting the way the world actually is.

Your mind might say, "Well, I don't like that! I don't like the way they said this or that." Ask yourself now, "Who doesn't like it? Who is judging and condemning? Who is

making up a story?  Who is caught by their attachment?"
"Well, 'I' am!"

It might be helpful here to give a definition of
attachment.  An attachment is anything we take personally,
any thought, any feeling, any sensation!  When we think
these thoughts or feelings are "mine", this is "me", this is
who "I" am, at that point, mind has become attached and
this causes craving to arise in your mind and body.

Craving always manifests as a tension or tightness in
both mind and body.  Craving is the "I" like it, "I" don't like
it mind - which arises in everyone's mind/body process.
Attachment is another word for craving and is the start of
all suffering.  When we see that everything that arises is
part of an impersonal process, then, we begin to understand
what it is like to see things with a clear observant mind.

Somebody might say something very innocently and you
hear it through your attachment and it's negative. This is
why we have to learn how to become aware of what is
happening all the time in our daily lives.

When you get finished sitting in your meditation for 30
minutes, 45 minutes, or for an hour and you start walking
around, what does your mind do?  It takes off just like it
always does.  It thinks about this.  It thinks about that.
This is just non-sense thoughts.

Most of us think those thoughts and those feelings that
arise are ours personally; that they are not just random
things.  But, in truth, if you feed any kind of a thought or
feeling with your attention, you make it bigger and more

intense. When you realize that you are causing your own suffering, you have to forgive yourself for doing that.

This means saying, "I forgive myself for not understanding. I forgive myself completely." Of course, your mind is going to take off again and say, "Aah! This is stupid! This is nothing. This isn't real. This isn't what is actually happening. 'I' don't want to do this!"

Every one of those thoughts is an attachment, isn't it? Every one of those thoughts has craving in it, doesn't it? Every one of those thoughts is causing you suffering, right?

Because of this, you have to recognize that you are doing this to yourself and let go of those thoughts. That's just nonsense stuff anyway. It doesn't have anything to do with what you are doing and where you are right now. Once you know this, you forgive yourself for not understanding; for causing yourself pain; for causing other people pain. YOU REALLY FORGIVE.

Take a look at when you are walking from here to there. What are you doing with your mind? "Ho Hum. Thinking about this, and, I gotta do that, and, I have to go talk to that person, and, I have to do this." All of that's non-sense!

Now, this doesn't mean that you can't plan what you need to do next. You can. But just do that planning one time as your primary topic in the present moment. After you make up your mind what the plan is, you don't have to think about it anymore. Repeating it, rolling it around again; all of that is just part of your old habitual tendency (bhava in Pāli). It is your old conditioned thoughts and feelings, and taking them personally and causing yourself pain and suffering.

# CHAPTER FOUR – Daily Practice

Including the exercise of forgiveness in your daily activity is by far the most important part of this meditation. You forgive yourself continually, for not understanding, for getting caught up in this or that, for taking things personally. How many times have you found yourself doing this? "Hey! I don't like the way you said that." Ask yourself. WHO doesn't like what? "Well, you said something that was hurtful." To WHOM?

You need to stop and realize that you're taking all this stuff personally and it's not really personal. It's just stuff that happens. Forgive it! Forgive it even when you're walking along a road and you happen to kick a rock and it hurts. Forgive the pain for being there! Your job is to keep your mind forgiving all the time. That's what Mindfulness of Forgiveness Meditation practice is all about. The technique is not just about when you are sitting. This is a life practice. This is an all-the-time practice.

If you want to really begin to change, you have to be willing to go through the forgiveness sincerely, because it will help you change a lot. You have to have patience and it helps to have a sense of humor about just how dumb mind can be.  The more you smile and laugh the easier the meditation becomes.

# CHAPTER FIVE - Finding Balance

Whenever you personally continue to think about this and that, to judge this and condemn that, you are constantly causing yourself suffering. You don't need to do that. You want to argue with other people about your attachments? What's the point? When you really start practicing forgiveness for yourself, or forgiveness for another person, your mind starts to get into balance and your sense of humor begins to change. This is equanimity. Then you don't take thoughts, feelings and sensations and all this other stuff personally.

When you practice in this way, you are seeing life for what it is and allowing it to be there. It's not worth going over it in your mind, and over it, and over it, and over it. It's not worth it. It's a waste of time. It's a waste of effort. Every time you have a repeat thought, you are attached. You're identifying with that thought and you're taking it personally and that is again the cause of suffering. What you are seeing here is the Second Noble Truth. You are witnessing how Craving, taking it personally is the cause of suffering. And you can't blame anybody else for it. It's yours. You are doing it all to yourself. "WELL, they said this!"

So what?

Others may have their opinion. That doesn't mean 'I' have to listen to them. I don't have to take it in personally and analyze whether it's correct or not, because it doesn't matter. The more you forgive in your daily life and daily activities, the easier it is to forgive the big things that happened in the past.

# CHAPTER SIX - Persistence

When you're doing the Forgiveness Meditation while you're sitting, you're staying with one of the suggested statements. You stay with that one statement until you internally feel, "YES, I really do forgive myself for not understanding." It's important to work this through.

To really forgive can take awhile. It's not just some quick fix to do in one sitting and then you come in and say, "OK, now I'm done!", or you say, "I've already done that". Doing that is not where you're going to get real change. Nope. You still have your attachments there. You still have to continually forgive yourself for not understanding, forgive yourself for making a mistake. That is what not understanding is about. You have to forgive yourself for judging, for condemning, for analyzing, for thinking, for getting angry. Forgive everything, all of the time.

When I started to do the forgiveness meditation, which, I did personally for myself for two years, because I wanted to make sure I really understood this meditation, I went through major changes. There were major changes; major personality changes. If you want that for yourself, you have to have that kind of patience.

This idea of, "Well, I've already forgiven this person or that person", that simply isn't it. A little later on you figure out that you're talking about how YOU didn't like this or that from them! Ah! Guess what? Who hasn't finished their forgiveness meditation? YOU haven't forgiven yourself, or that other person!

# CHAPTER SEVEN - Going Deeper

When you start to go deeper in your meditation, staying with the forgiveness, and you do forgive yourself for making mistakes, there can come a time when somebody comes up into your mind that you need to forgive.

When this happens, you realize that you did not ask them to come up. You do not stop and say, "Well, I need this person to come up." They came up by themselves.

As soon as that person comes up, you start forgiving them, for not understanding. It doesn't matter what they did in the past. All of your thoughts, all of your opinions of what they did in the past just keep bringing up more suffering.

These thoughts come up because of your attachment. "I didn't like that! I didn't want that to happen! They are a dirty no good so and so because they did that to me." Can you guess where the attachment is? Guess where the idea comes from that I can blame somebody else for my own suffering? The only person you can blame for your suffering is yourself. Why? Because, YOU are the one that took it personally. You're the one who had an opinion about it. You're the one that used your habitual tendencies over and over again to justify the idea that I'm right and you're wrong. That's how we cause our own suffering.

The forgiveness meditation helps you let go of that opinion, that idea, that attachment, and feel some relief. Because some past person did or said something that caused anger, resentment, jealousy, pain or whatever the catch of the day was – it can have a real tendency for your mind to get caught up in thinking about that past event.

This is called getting caught by the story. You need to use the 6R's and then go back to your forgiveness statement. It doesn't matter how many times the story arises, please use the 6R's and then forgive again. The story's emotion will fade away after you do this enough. This is where patience is needed.

# CHAPTER EIGHT - Letting Go

When you see someone else come up in your mind, somebody you really had a rough time with and you didn't like it; someone you started hating for whatever reason, you forgive them. With your mind's eye, you look them straight in their eye and you tell them sincerely: "I forgive you for not understanding the situation, I forgive you for causing me pain, I forgive you completely."

Now, keep that person in your heart and radiate Forgiveness to them. If your mind has a distraction and it pulls you away from that; you might hear in your mind, "No, I don't, that no good so and so. I won't forgive him!" Using the 6R's, let go of this and come back and say, "I do forgive you."

It has to be sincere. "Well, I'm not going to forgive that dirty no good so and so." Why not? "Because, they caused 'ME' suffering!" Oops! WHO caused who suffering? YOU caused your own self suffering because you took it personally, and YOU reinforced that with a lot of thoughts and opinions and ideas about why that was wrong.

In other words, you were caught in your craving, your own clinging, your habitual tendencies and that leads to more and more dissatisfaction, aversion, pain and suffering.

# CHAPTER NINE - Relief

It's really important to realize that this is not an easy practice. It's hard to forgive someone when they have really caused you harm. Take a woman that has been raped or a man who has been beaten and robbed. It's hard to forgive the person who raped them or beat them because they have been violated. But, holding onto their hatred of that person is keeping them attached. It doesn't matter what the action was. It doesn't matter what happened in the past. What matters is what you are doing with what you have in your mind right now.

To completely develop this practice to the highest level means that you keep forgiving and forgiving! Over and over. With your mind's eye, you look them straight in the eye and you say, "I really do forgive you." And your mind says, "NO, I DON'T" And you let that go, and 6R, and come back. You say, "I really do forgive you." Then take that person and put them in your heart and continue to radiate forgiveness to them. How long do you do that? As long as it takes.

For some attachments, one or two sittings is all you will need. Some other attachments, might take a week; might take two weeks or even longer. Who knows? It doesn't matter.  If you need time, you can take time! You have all the time there is.

You will feel a very, very strong sense of relief when you let go of the hatred you have towards these people.  Then any time you think of them, you kind of think of them with a mind that says, "Well, they made a mistake, they didn't know what they were doing. It's ok."

That's how you let go of an attachment (craving).  That's how you let go of the pain of that past situation.  This doesn't mean that the person who was violated is going to go up and hug the person who did that to them.  They would avoid them because they know there is a possibility of personal harm.  But they don't hate them anymore.  They don't think about it anymore. They have let it go.

That's what the forgiveness is all about.  It's about letting go.  You are giving up old dissatisfaction and dislike. You are developing a mind that says, "Well that's ok. You can be like that." That is not taking it personally.

While I was in Asia on a three month retreat. There was a water well pump that was drilling for water right outside of the meditation hall. Three months of an old clanky motor running from 8 o'clock in the morning until 6 o'clock at night. This can happen, you know? One continuous noise! It was really loud and really annoying, but, it was just sound. That's all it was. I realized that it was not "MY" sound. "My" dislike of that sound wasn't going to change that sound. "My" criticizing of the person that started the motor wasn't going to make that sound any different.

Do you see where all the attachments are in this example? The exercise here is accepting the fact that sound is here, and it's ok for sound to be here. It has to be ok, because, that's what's in the present moment. That's the truth [Dhamma]. Accepting the present moment is accepting the Dhamma just as it is.

Whenever there is a disturbance, forgive the disturbance continually in your mind. FORGIVE. Smile. Forgive yourself for not understanding. That is how we work with forgiveness in daily life. I forgive myself for wanting things to be more perfect than they are. I forgive myself for making mistakes. I forgive myself for being angry, and, disliking this or that. Now we see that the forgiveness is not just one statement, it can be many. We take each of these statements into the practice and use them one by one.

# CHAPTER FIFTEEN – *No Mantras*

While you're doing your sitting practice, once again, you just want to take one statement of forgiveness at a time. Stay with just one.  Remember that this is not a mantra. You don't surface say this and think about something else either.  It has to be sincere.  "I really do forgive myself for making mistakes or for not understanding or whatever". It's important to be sincere when you do this.

The more you can continually forgive, with your daily activities, with your sitting, with your walking meditation, whatever you happen to be doing; you need to realize that this is what meditation is really about.

Meditation is not about gaining some super-human state of mind.  It's not just about bliss.  It is more productive than that.  It's about learning how you cause your own suffering and how to let go of that suffering.  The deeper super-human states of meditation will come up by themselves when we clear our minds and simply allow this to happen.  You don't have to personally do anything.

The more you clear yourself, the more you clear your mind of judgments, opinions, concepts, ideas, and the more the early texts; using it with any meditation you are doing, this is one of the fastest ways for all people to see clearly what is really going on and to reach this kind of destination where there can be happiness and Peace.

In sutta number 21 of the Majjhima Nikaya, as translated by Bhikkhu Bodhi, within The Middle Length Sayings' and published by Wisdom Publications, it gives us some excellent advice that I would like to share with you now. It says:

"There are these five courses of speech that others may use when they address you, their speech may be timely or untimely, true or untrue, gentle or harsh, connected with good or connected with harm, spoken with a mind of loving-kindness or with inner hatred.

"This is how i should train: My mind shall be unaffected and I will utter no evil words; I shall abide compassionate for their welfare, with a mind of loving-kindness, without inner hate. I shall abide pervading that person (whoever you talk with) with a mind imbued with loving-kindness (and forgiveness) and starting with him, I shall abide pervading the all-encompassing world with a mind imbued with loving-kindness, abundant, exalted, immeasurable, without hostility and without ill-will". That is how I should train.

Please use this Forgiveness Meditation often and train your mind to be happy!

# APPENDIX 1 - Review of T.W.I.M.

A quick brush-up on:

"Simple, Easy to Understand Mindfulness"

"Tranquil Wisdom Insight Meditation" (TWIM) training is the basic framework for all of our meditation methods and their resultant success.

**MEDITATION** is "observing mind's attention as it moves moment-to-moment in order to see precisely 'HOW' suffering happens.   Too understand this, we study the impersonal process of Human Cognition.  This reveals HOW we experience our environment.  Seeing and understanding 'HOW' mind' works when attention moves from one thing to another is what this ancient practice is about.  This leads us to a more impersonal perspective so that we do not suffer so deeply while living life.

**MINDFULNESS** is what keeps this observation going all the time.  Tranquil Wisdom Insight Meditation (TWIM) is a reclaimed ancient guidance system with 6 simple steps to keep our meditation going strong. Mindfulness helps us develop our observation skill so we can keep the 6R's going. Mindfulness tells us what to do.  It helps us RECOGNIZE when tension changes in our bodies as mind's attention moves away from our object of meditation or from our task in life. We REMEMBER [use mindfulness] to observe mind's attention moving and then the practice cycle can begin to help us make a correction and continue meditating. So, Mindfulness is the fuel just like gas keeps a car going. Without Mindfulness, everything stops! If we persistently keep going, the meditation will relieve suffering of all kinds. So, to begin the cycle "smoothly" one must start the engine and have lots of gas (mindfulness) in the tank! Now we continue on with the steps of the Meditation Cycle.

**RECOGNIZE**: This means we learn to recognize any movement of mind's attention away from an object of meditation, such as the breath, sending out of Metta, practicing Forgiveness or, any task in daily life that you are doing.

We can learn to notice a slightly tense sensation as mind's attention barely begins to move toward an arising phenomena. Pleasant or painful feeling can occur at any one of the six sense doors. Any sight, sound, odor, taste, touch, or thought can cause a pulling sensation to begin. With careful non-judgmental observation, the meditator notices a slight tightening sensation. Watch carefully. RECOGNIZING this early movement is vital to successful meditation. One then continues on to...

**RELEASE**: When a thought or feeling arises, the meditator RELEASES it, let's it be there without giving any more attention to it. We do not feed it attention. The content of the distraction is not important at all, but the mechanics of HOW it arose **ARE** important! Just let go of any tightening around it. Let it be there without placing attention on it. Without attention, the tightness will pass away.  Then Mindfulness reminds the meditator to...

**RELAX**: After releasing the feeling or sensation, and allowing it to be there without trying to control it, there is a subtle, barely noticeable tension in mind/body. This is why the extra TRANQUILIZATION] or RELAX step is being pointed out in the Buddha's instructions.  It turns out that within the Ānāpānasati instructions, the tranquilization step mentioned was a separate independent step. Over time this instruction has become blurred.

### PLEASE, DON'T SKIP THIS STEP!

A motor can't run smoothly without oil in the engine. This is the oil! Without performing this relaxation step every time in the practice cycle, the meditator will not experience the reality of the state of cessation of suffering as a real state.  The tension was caused by CRAVING and this cuts us off from discovering a ceasing of the suffering.  We cannot feel the relief when the tightness falls away if we do not perform this relax step. This is cutting edge.

Note: *Craving always manifests as a tightness or tension in both one's mind and body.*

One has a momentary opportunity to see and experience the true nature and relief that comes from cessation of the tightness within suffering while performing the RELEASE/RELAX steps. Notice this relief.  Mindfulness now reminds us to...

**RE-SMILE**: If you have listened to the meditation instructions at our website you might remember hearing how smiling is an important aspect for this meditation. Smiling in your mind, in your eyes, in your heart, and on your lips helps sharpen awareness, become alert, agile and more observant. Getting serious, tensing up or frowning causes mind to become heavy, dull and slow.    Mindfulness falls down. Insights become difficult to experience. This slows understanding the truth of HOW things work.    So, Re-smile. Start again. Keeping up your humor, sense of fun, and exploration is important.    After re-smiling, mindfulness recalls the next step...

**RETURN or RE-DIRECT**: Gently re-direct mind's attention back to the object of meditation that is the **breath and relaxing**, or **metta and relaxing**. Continue on with a gentle collected mind and use your object of meditation as a "home base", a re-centering point during the practice.    This will help you stay in the present moment In daily life.  If you are pulled off task, one returns mind's attention back to releasing, relaxing, and re-smiling into whatever task you are doing in life.

Imagine, for a moment, you are a resting under an Apple Tree, not serious and tense about anything.  As you lean back against the tree, not thinking about anything, you attain a pleasant abiding with a light mind.  This is what first happened to the Buddha when he was very young while sitting under a Rose-Apple Tree during a Harvest Festival his Father was attending.

Want to see things more clearly?  Be still. Lighten up.  SMILE.  This opens the door to a happier life.  If you forget to Release/Relax, don't punish yourself.  Instead of punishing or criticizing yourself, be kind and forgive yourself.

Sometimes people say this practice cycle is simpler than expected!  Reclaiming this practice develops more effective focus for daily tasks, more balance, deeper sleep, and people become more easy going and happy.    The meditator becomes more efficient at whatever they are doing in life. Because they discover more about HOW things actually work, this helps them to have less fear and hesitation in life.      Mindfulness then helps with a final recollection to...

**REPEAT**:  this practice cycle to retrain mind to relieve suffering in this lifetime.  Repeating the "6R's cycle" over and over again trains mind to let go of a lot of suffering as we realize the meaning of the Four Noble Truths
1) We see and experience for ourselves what suffering actually is [First Noble Truth];
2) We notice the cause which is becoming personally involved it causing  tension and tightness [Second Noble Truth];
3) We experience what the cessation of suffering feels like [Third Noble Truth]; and
4) We discover a way to increase this comfortable state of the cessation of suffering. [Fourth Noble Truth].

This happens each time we Release an arising feeling, Relax and Re-smile.  Notice the Relief. Keep it going and give your smiles away!  That is the entire practice in a nutshell. Now go for it!

# *About the Author*

The principle guiding Teacher is our Abbot Most Venerable "Bhante" Vimalaramsi

Mahāthera; Trained through the Burmese Theravāda School and Mahāsi System of training. But now a declared Suttavadin!

Founder: United International Buddha Dhamma Society 2003, Abbot for Dhamma Sukha Meditation Center/ Anāthapiṇḍika's Study Park Complex 2005-Present, Official Founder and Spiritual head for the Buddhist American Forest Tradition (New Suttavada Sect). Bhante is Head Teacher for Tranquil Wisdom Insight Meditation and he oversees the research, practice, preservation, and teaching of early foundation Buddhist teachings as found in the Pali texts.

He has been a monk since 1986, with over 40 years of practice and with over 12 years of that in Asia. He holds the first life-time position given to a Representative for Buddhists in the USA; to the World Buddhist Council based in Kobe, Japan. 2006 - Questions may be sent to Bhante Vimalaramsi via info@dhammasukha.org

# *Other Resources*

Dhamma Sukha Meditation Center website:
    www.dhammasukha.org.

Vimalaraṁsi, Bhante, *Meditation is Life, Life is Meditation*
    (CreateSpace, 2014).

Vimalaraṁsi, Bhante, *Breath of Love* (Ehipassiko Foundation
    of Indonesia, 2012).

Vimalaraṁsi, Bhante, *Moving Dhamma, Volume 1.*
    (CreateSpace, 2012).


Dhamma Sukha Meditation Center

8218 County Road 204

Annapolis, MO 63620

info@dhammasukha.org

# *Sharing Merit*

May Suffering ones by suffering free
and the fear-struck, fearless be,
May the grieving shed all grief,
and may all beings find relief.

May all beings share this merit that we have thus acquired,
for the acquisition of all kinds of happiness.
May beings inhabiting Space and Earth,
Devas and Nagas of mighty power,
share this merit of ours.

May they long protect the Buddha's Dispensation.

SADHU, SADHU, SADHU

CPSIA information can be obtained
at www.ICGtesting.com
Printed in the USA
BVOW03s1253201217
503281BV00021B/83/P

# CHAPTER SIXTEEN – Blame Game

Your Forgiveness Meditation is more than just about old attachments like, "Well, when I was five years old, Little Johnny, he beat me up and I've hated him ever since then." See how this is about you and uncovering this attachment and how you hold onto it, and how you cause yourself pain because of that attachment?

Most especially these days, people are really big on blaming everybody but themselves for their pain, and, the question here should be, is that working with reality or not? It's easy to say, "YOU caused me pain. I don't like you." But, did someone else cause you pain? Or did I just say something and you had another kind of an opinion, and, judged and condemned whatever I said, and then, your aversion came up, and the dislike of the whole situation, and now, you're off to the races and you're a thousand miles away.

You are causing yourself pain and you're running into your thinking, "But, I'm only thinking and analyzing." Ha ha ha ha ha! You're attached! You think, "This attachment won't hurt me so much if I keep distracted. I can keep MY opinions, and my ideas about the way things are supposed to be, and then, I don't have to change!" But, you're fooling you accept what's happening in the present moment, the more joyful life becomes. The easier life becomes.

What's that you are saying now? "Well, I have this habit of always analyzing and thinking." OK, let it go. "BUT I have been doing this my whole life." So? Hey! Forgive yourself for not understanding. Forgive yourself for analyzing.

There can be a strong attachment to wanting to analyze. That's the Western disease. "I want to know how everything works." You don't learn how things work by thinking about them. You let go and relax to see how things work when you forgive, and, you let go and relax to develop space in your mind to observe how they work.

The truth is that, in meditation, thinking mind, analyzing mind is incredibly slow. The aware mind is incredibly fast. It's extraordinary! You just can't get there with a lot of words in the way. You can't have opinions in the way. They will block you. They will stop you from seeing the way things truly are.

understand what you are doing. It's ok that they don't understand. It's ok that they don't know where you are or what you are doing. They can judge you, they can condemn you, they can cause all kinds of distractions, and that's fine. They can do that. BUT, as for you, you can forgive them for it.

As you are forgiving them, you are letting go of the attachment to the way 'I' think things are supposed to be. Not understanding can be a really big thing. Because we don't understand so much; we have our own opinions and ideas of the way things are supposed to work; that can be a problem. We get caught up by assumption. That's it, isn't it?

What happens when things don't match your idea of the way things are supposed to work? What then? You may find yourself fighting with REALITY which is the truth, the Dhamma of the present moment! You're not accepting the reality that's right there in front of you. You begin judging and condemning, and, most often, blaming somebody else for, disturbing you.

Well, I'm sorry... They're *not* disturbing your practice. THEY ARE PART OF THE PRACTICE! There's no such thing as something else, or someone else, disturbing MY PRACTICE. It's only me fighting with what is real, the REALITY, the Dhamma of the present moment, not liking this or that, and next, I am blaming somebody else OR something else for the cause of that...

# CHAPTER FOURTEEN – Forgive it!

What about sounds disturbing us while we practice? Sometimes, in a retreat, if you are concentrating too hard you can observe what can happen. You could get SO upset if there is even one squeak of a door, or someone is walking by too heavily near you, or breathing too loudly. You might jump up thinking "OH! You disturbed my practice!"

Do you begin to see how ridiculous this actually is? What is happening here is that the present moment produced a noise; and there was noise, and then, mind came up and said, "I don't like this. That's not supposed to be there." "I want to complain to somebody, and make them stop so MY mind can be peaceful!" What is actually happening is concentration is out of balance with mindfulness. Concentration is too strong and mindfulness is too weak. Hahaha! How crazy is that?

If you can't accept what's happening in the present moment, with a balanced mind, there will be suffering. OK! So! There's a noise. "There's somebody talking!" So? It doesn't matter just as long as you have mindfulness and equanimity in your mind. When balance is in your mind, if there is a noise, that's just fine. And? You can do your forgiveness meditation!

# CHAPTER TWELVE - Success!

After you forgive that person, you stay with them; you stay with that person that's come up into your mind until you feel like, "Enough! I don't have to do this anymore. I really have forgiven you." At that point, with your mind's eye, you look them straight in the eye, and you stop verbalizing and you hear them say back to you: "I forgive you too."

Wow! Now this is different, isn't it? It's kind of remarkable. You have this feeling of being forgiven as well as you forgiving them! You've forgiven yourself for making mistakes, for not understanding. You've forgiven that other person for making mistakes, for not understanding, or causing pain, whatever you want using the statement that really makes it true for you. And, now, you hear them say "I forgive you."

There is a real sense of relief. Wow! What happens in your mind now is that JOY comes up in your mind. You feel light. You feel really happy. Happier then you ever felt before. You didn't realize you were carrying these big bundles of rocks on your shoulders, holding you down, did you? And now, you have put them down. When you forgive,

And what is that guilt? Non-forgiveness. That's an example of your mind grabbing onto what's happening and saying, "I really screwed up and I need to punish myself for that." That's what your mind is saying. Now do you see what you can do about this? Right! The more you become serious with your daily life, the more attachments you will have. The less equanimity, the less mental balance you will have in your life.

There is no question about it. You're on these roller coasters; emotional roller coasters, up and down, up and down, up and down. When you start forgiving more, those high high's, and low low's start to turn into little waves. You still have some. But you don't get caught for as long. You just stop and say, "This just isn't important enough to get upset about."

happened; it's in the past; it's no big deal." This is what forgiveness is all about.

# CHAPTER ELEVEN - Daily Life

How can this practice affect your daily life?  This is a good question.   You're more open, you're more accepting.  You're not judging.  You're not condemning.  You're not disliking, because as you see that tightness of mind coming up in you, and you go, "Oops! I forgive you for not understanding this one!", and you smile.  You let it go.

One of the hardest things a guiding teacher has to do is to teach people that 'Life is supposed to be fun'.  It's a game!  Keep it light!  If you, play with your mind and your attachments that means you are not being attached to them so much.  As you play with them, you're not taking them so seriously anymore.  When you don't take them seriously, they're easier to let go of.

That's what the Buddha was teaching us!  He was teaching us how to have an uplifted mind all of the time; how to be able to be light with your thoughts, with your feelings, and your ideas, and your past actions.

Yes.  It's true.  On some occasion you made a mistake.  Well?  Ok!  Welcome to the human race!  I don't know of anyone who hasn't made a mistake and felt guilty about it.  Sure they do.

# *CHAPTER SEVENTEEN – Be Happy!*

In summary, BUDDHISM is about realizing that you need to have a balanced and mindful mind, that doesn't have high emotions in it, that doesn't' have attachments in it, so that you can see things clearly and discover real happiness and contentment in daily life.

BUDDHISM is about seeing the way things truly are; gaining knowledge by seeing for yourself how you are the cause of your own pain. It's about taking personal responsibility and doing the work needed to find this kind of mindfulness, balance and understanding.

Mindfulness of Forgiveness Meditation trains us to recognize clearly when suffering arises [First Noble Truth]; to notice how we get personally involved with it and make it bigger which causes more suffering in life [Second Noble Truth]; and to escape this dangerous trap by using the 6R's and seeing how it disappears [Third Noble Truth]; This meditation opens the way for clear understanding and relief [Fourth Noble Truth].

The end-result creates the space we need in our mind so that we begin to respond to life instead of re-acting. Using the 6R's, which fulfills the practice of Right Effort found in yourself. Change is the only way to free mind. Meditation is about positive change.

mind-states into new wholesome tendencies. Be kind to yourself and take your time.

The whole point of the Meditation is LEARNING HOW TO CHANGE. Learning how to let go of those old non-sense ideas and thoughts and develop new ideas and thoughts that make you happy and make other people around you happy too. That's the whole reason for the precepts. They outline an option for us to follow so we gain balance in our life.

Let's take a quick look at the precepts. Do not kill any living beings on purpose. Don't take what is not freely given to you (no stealing). Don't engage in wrong sexual activity with another person's mate or a person too young living with their parents. In short, don't do anything that will cause mental or physical harm to any other human being. Don't engage in telling lies, using harsh language, gossip, or slander. Lastly, don't take recreational drugs or alcohol because these will weaken mind and the tendency to break the other precepts is stronger!

These precepts are like an ultimate operational manual for life. If you keep them well, then you get the most out of your life, they make you, and others around you happy. The more you can continually follow them, the better your frame of mind will become. You will more easily forgive that other person, your mind will become softer towards that person, and you will feel more relief.

What happens is, after you practice this way for a while, then you go "Ah, I do, I really do forgive you!" and there's no, energy behind it at all. It's just like, "yeah, this

# CHAPTER TEN - Obstacles

The biggest part of the Mindfulness of Forgiveness Meditation is learning how to let go of your personal opinions, ideas, concepts, stories. You might stay with a person for a long period of time because of your opinions and your attachment to this.

Every time you are doing any walking or sitting meditation, keep forgiving them over and over again. Your mind might get bored with that and say, "OH, I don't want to do this anymore!"

Well that's another kind of attachment, isn't it? So, what do you do with that? You have to get through it by forgiving the boredom for being there. That's ok. Your mind is tricky. It's going to try to distract you any way it can. It'll bring up any kind of feelings and thoughts and ideas to distract you, because, it doesn't like the idea of giving up attachments. Your mind really feels comfortable, holding onto attachments.

We need to go easy on ourselves as we develop this practice. After all, how many years did it take us to build up our habits [bhava]? It takes patience to move in the opposite direction now and to change those unwholesome

# CHAPTER THIRTEEN – Not Easy

This practice has NO simple, easy, fast-fix here!  You can't just buy the solution this time at the Mall either.  You have to patiently continue this practice all the time until you release the unwholesome mind-states which are your old habitual tendencies of mind.

Depending how attached you are to the idea that a person wronged you, or the idea of how badly you screwed up, this leads you into "I can never forgive myself."  Until you finally go through this process of forgiveness, you will not be free of this burden.

You WILL know when you have gone entirely through the Mindfulness of Forgiveness Meditation because then you will be free and you will see clearly this is how Forgiveness really works.  Are you done?  You don't have to have anybody to tell you that this worked.  You'll know!

The daily continuous work of this practice is most important.  When you are walking from one place to another, I don't care what you are doing.  Any kind of distraction that comes up, forgive it.  Smile.  If a person comes up to you and they start talking and you don't want to talk, FORGIVE THEM.  They don't understand.  They don't the heaviness of those hard feelings and "rocks" disappear. You feel light. "Oh My! This REALLY is great stuff!"

It takes a lot of work, but, it's worth it. It's not easy. Why isn't it easy? Because of the amount of attachment we have when we begin. You keep doing the meditation and when you get done with one person, you go back to yourself. You repeat: "I forgive myself for making mistakes. I forgive myself for not understanding." You stay with yourself until somebody else comes up into your mind. You keep on doing that until your mind says, "OK. I've done it. Everything is good. There's nobody else. Enough!"

At this time, you can switch back to your Mindfulness of Loving-Kindness meditation and make it your primary formal practice. Now you can understand why Mindfulness of Forgiveness Meditation is definitely part of Loving-Kindness. How can you ever practice Loving-Kindness if you have hatred? You can't. This practice releases the Hatred.